# "Things Your Phone Can Never! Tell You"

## For Generation Z

Sue Davidoff

WESTBOW
PRESS®
A DIVISION OF THOMAS NELSON
& ZONDERVAN

WestBow Press books may be ordered through booksellers or by contacting:

WestBow Press
A Division of Thomas Nelson & Zondervan
1663 Liberty Drive
Bloomington, IN 47403
www.westbowpress.com
1 (866) 928-1240

ISBN: 978-1-9736-5100-0 (sc)
ISBN: 978-1-9736-5099-7 (e)

Library of Congress Control Number: 2019900700

Print information available on the last page.

WestBow Press rev. date: 01/18/2019

# Contents

# Foreword

Today may be the most important day of all your life, and of all your days . . . . . IF you can find "it", that very thing that you are looking for, even now, that thing you know is out there.

If you could find "it", it WOULD BE the most important day of all your life.

_Search as you may on your phone or I-Pad - trust me - it's not there._

If you can find "it" in this book, my labors will not have been in vain; this means, that all my hard work will help you find it.

I PRAY THAT YOU WILL FIND THIS BOOK
AND
THAT THIS BOOK – WILL FIND YOU.

YOU
ARE THE REASON FOR
THIS BOOK, AND SO
THIS BOOK IS DEDICATED TO YOU!

_____

(Write your name above on the line)

(And underline and make notes
for yourself in your book)

THIS IS — YOUR BOOK!

# 1

# Stop!

. . . . . reading, that is, right after you read this 1st chapter, and go back and "follow the prompts".

Carry the book with you, and GO OUTSIDE, but only if you feel safe going outside. If not, you can just picture this chapter in your mind. Now get up, even if it's cold outside or 105 degrees in the summer; go outside even if you don't want to leave the nice warm heat inside or the nice cool air-conditioning.

Just do it — go outside. When you are outside, LOOK UP. What do you see? The sun? Clouds? Mountains? A rainbow? Rain or snow? The sun "coming up" or "going down"? The moon? Stars? Other planets? The universe? Actually you can't see all the universe, because it goes way beyond what human beings can see, even with their most powerful telescopes! Maybe it's a cloudy or foggy day or night, and you can't see very much, but for sure you can see the sky!

Do you see a BEAUTIFUL PAINTING (of many different colors and shades) painted all across the sky, or can you just see all fluffy clouds across the sky? Or do you see the black and white sparkles of the night and a golden yellow moon?

Because you are looking up, God is looking down – on you. He is sooo happy you are looking up – and noticing His artwork and colors all across the sky. He would absolutely love it IF you spoke out loud and told Him how beautiful it all is! You could say, out loud, "Lord, what YOU have painted across the sky is AWESOME and something no human being could ever do. THANK YOU for letting me see it – just now."

It would make Him even happier if you told Him you will do it again. You may be THE ONLY PERSON in the world to be noticing all of His hard work He put into the sky at that very moment, in that very place from where you are standing.

Of course, most everyone else is watching TV right now, eating, playing pretend "games" on their phones and I-Pads, doing "Facebook", or ordering and buying even more stuff "online", that they already know will not make them any happier. They are buying more stuff mainly because they are just plain bored. They already know that when the brown box arrives on their front porch, they will feel even sadder, because the "it" they are looking for – is not in the box.

Most everyone else is "so busy" doing their other things, that they never even stop to notice what God is doing . . .

# BUT NOT YOU.

Sue Davidoff

Aren't you kind of wondering now . . . . .

. . . . . what's on the "<u>other side</u>" of the sky? "<u>Up above</u>" it all? since you are standing below it?

OH, BEFORE I FORGET, YOU
CAN GO BACK INSIDE NOW!

:)

# 2

# On The Other Side
# of The Sky

. . . . . the name of the country God and His son, Jesus, live in is <u>Heaven. It's the country on the other side of the sky.</u> That's their country address.

No one knows the names of the streets and house addresses up there, but for sure they are there!

We do know about the streets and roads, because they are paved in gold! not concrete or asphalt. Sounds like God is pretty rich, doesn't it? Can you even imagine the whole city you live in, and drive your cars in, being paved in gold? Maybe there aren't cars in Heaven, maybe everyone just walks or flies everywhere?

We do know about the houses though. THEY ARE ALL MANSIONS ! which is VERY EXPENSIVE real estate. No "low income" housing or creepy neighborhoods (that feel dangerous) are up there, unlike down here on this side. And no "high income" housing either up there, because rich neighborhoods down here can also feel creepy and dangerous, because thieves may want to get inside your nice house, and steal all your stuff you've bought "on-line". NO CREEPY RICH OR POOR NEIGHBORHOODS IN HEAVEN, BECAUSE THERE ARE NO THIEVES OR BAD SCARY PEOPLE UP IN HEAVEN, BECAUSE THE LORD IS THE KING THERE AND HE DOES NOT ALLOW IT! That's right, HE IS TOTALLY IN CHARGE, YOU CAN BE SURE OF THAT!

Back to the "mansions". They are all "customs", which means that each one is custom-built and prepared with all the furnishings inside, all picked out and prepared "ahead of time" —for whoever it's built for – BEFORE they arrive. And the landscaping is absolutely gorgeous – trees, rivers, "green belts" that make even our most beautiful and expensive golf courses down here look – substandard.

But the most wonderful treasure of all is that The Lord and His son, Jesus, live there, and because of this, no one is ever sad up there! In Heaven, God Himself wipes away everyones' tears from their eyes, and there is no more death, no more sorrow, no more crying, no more pain – in Heaven.

The country on the other side is very different from the countries we know down here.

# 3

# Have You Ever Wondered

. . . . . how you got here? Surely, you have wondered about this – sometime. Yes?

You got here because The Lord (God) made you and put you here! Adam and Eve were the first people He put here thousands of years ago, and we are all their descendants; however, He designed each one of us – to be different – from everyone else and with unique gifts.

Someone who built the first "Apple" watch with internet access had to put a ton of time and thought into it, to create a thing so complex and yet so small.

But you are even so much more complex than a fully loaded "Apple" watch. If there has to be a creator of the "Apple" watch, there HAS TO BE a creator — of you! This creator has to make a human being out of another human being, then add a beating heart and all of the complex systems that must work together, put a soul inside of it, then breathe into the shell and working systems, so that it all comes "alive". Then give this magnificent creation – A SPIRIT THAT WILL LIVE FOREVER.

The shell of this one-of-a-kind creation could maybe be copied and built out of plastic and metal, and be controlled by computer "chips", whereby the shell of the human being would respond to the programmed "commands". But the copied plastic human being would not be "alive" or have a soul or a spirit; it would only be a computer programmed "robot".

But the Lord didn't want to make a bunch of robots that He could sell and get money for, because remember He is a very rich king, and He doesn't need any earthly money.

<u>HE WENT TO ALL THE TIME AND TROUBLE TO MAKE EACH ONE OF US, BECAUSE HE WANTED SOMEONE TO LOVE – AND TO LOVE HIM BACK – AND HE WANTED SOMEONE HE COULD SPEND TIME WITH AND HANG OUT WITH.</u>

But how do you get someone to first of all, even notice that you even exist? How do you get someone to want to hang out with you and spend time with you? Get to know you? How do you get someone you love to WANT TO TALK TO YOU, and even more importantly, how do you get this other person to LOVE YOU BACK?

It certainly wouldn't mean very much to you if you knew the other person was just a robot that you could program, would it? Actually, it wouldn't mean anything at all, because the other person would just be responding to your programmed commands. Would this be much of a friend? I think not!

But God is soooo smart, He knew the ONLY WAY TO KNOW if someone He made would love Him back, was to . . . . .

GIVE THE ONE HE CREATED THE FREEDOM TO LOVE – OR NOT LOVE – HIM BACK. THIS WOULD BE ABSOLUTELY THE ONLY WAY HE COULD KNOW FOR SURE WHO WOULD LOVE HIM BACK.

But The Lord also knew that He would be taking a big chance, once He gave His creation, the freedom to choose. Sometimes this is called "free will" or "choices".

HE KNEW ONCE HE DID THIS, HE WOULD OPEN HIS OWN GOD-HEART UP TO A LOT OF PAIN AND HEARTACHE that He could have avoided altogether IF He had just made a bunch of robots. Pain and heartache IF the ones He created, gave Him the cold shoulder, didn't pay any attention to Him, and even made fun of Him, and were embarrassed to be associated with Him . . . . .

But then again, He would
never know for sure.

### BACK TO "HAVE YOU EVER WONDERED"

. . . . . how you got here . . . . .

God made you.

He put you here.

That's why you're here.

# 4

# What Would Be

. . . . . the 3 things you would pick — IF YOU COULD make 3 wishes AND have them all – come true? These kinds of wishes would be the "deep down in your heart" wishes, not the material kinds of wishes that you might have for things you see on TV ads or see "on-line".

When I was your age, I probably would have picked:

1. To not be so "afraid" anymore.

2. To not worry so much about what other people thought of me.

3. To not have to "die" myself, and for other people I love to not have to "die" either, so I wouldn't have to miss them; this wish would include my pets too!

WHAT IF, the "it" thing you are
looking for — could help make your
3 "heart" wishes come true?


WHAT IF IT COULD?

# 5

# The People He Put Here

. . . . . a very long time ago, made God so very sad, because they disobeyed Him in every way, and did everything that He did not want them to do. On purpose, they wanted to show God who was "in charge" down here! Only a few people on earth cared about God at all. He even sent many people (called prophets) to warn the people that God – would – have to punish them for their <u>bad things they did (called sins)</u>, in the hope that they would change and begin to obey God. But not only did they not listen to the prophets and even made fun of them, they killed them! It would have been so very hard to have been a prophet back then, with evil people making fun of you, and even trying to kill you! Through all this, God was very sorry that He had made mankind. But even sadder, because many of the few who loved Him – were now dead!

But for some strange reason, God – still – loved the people He had made, because they were still His kids. So He decided that He would do – only one – more thing to let them know how much He still loved them, but this one last thing would determine their destiny – forever – their past, their present, and their future. Whatever they chose – this one and only last time – would be their last "free will" decision to either disobey God or obey and love Him back. No more chances would be given, and no more lives would be sacrificed – after – this one last thing God would do for them.

# 6

# Because God Is
# Perfect and Holy

. . . . . (without sin), He will accept nothing less than perfect. People were dying all over the earth, and many were sick and poor, and afraid, and had miserable lives; and, they could not go to Heaven when they died, because they could not get in! They could not get in, because of their sins. Sins are the things that we do when we disobey God and that are wrong and bad – bad for other people, bad for us, and bad for God! Everyone who was – and who is – and who will ever be – a human being – has or will – sin. Therefore, no one could have God's help with them while they are here on earth, or when they die either, because there was no way God was going to let a bunch of "bratty", arrogant, disobedient kids come up to Heaven – to trash it all up with evil and sin. They had – already done that down here!

# 7

# Because They Could
# Not Save Themselves

. . . . . God would have to. He would have to make someone perfect and holy, just like Him. And he would have to make someone just like – us – the earth people. This perfect someone would have to "stand in" for all the others (sinners) on earth. HE WOULD HAVE TO PAY THE PRICE GOD SET — for all the sins of the world. The price He set would be – one sacrificial death for all the others. This would be – the last man He would send – and He would be – the only God-Man.

# 8

# Here's How It Happened

The Lord (God) picked out a young woman who had never had sex with a man before, a really precious young woman named Mary, who was actually engaged to be married to a man named Joseph. God sent an angel to tell Mary that He had chosen her (out of all the young women on earth) to be the mother of His Son who would save all the people on the earth from their sins.

She was so happy and overcome with joy and began to praise God in her heart and said beautiful things back to The Lord (God). And I feel sure she cried, because she was so honored that God had chosen – her. She said "yes" to God that she would do this for Him, and would be honored to carry His son in her womb and be his mother here on earth. So God put His God-seed inside her womb, and because God is not a man, there was no sex needed for Mary to become pregnant. The angel also told

Mary that her baby would be a son, and that His name would be – Jesus, the Son of God.

God also sent an angel to tell Joseph about Mary's pregnancy, so Joseph wouldn't think that Mary had had sex with someone else, other than him, when she became pregnant, and so that he would know that the baby would belong to God. This was very hard on Mary and Joseph, because they both knew that they had not had sex with each other, or Mary, with anyone else. They also knew that other people would spread rumors about Mary getting pregnant, even though she was not yet married. But Joseph loved Mary, and took care of her, inspite of all the shame they both endured for the 9 months she was pregnant (and really for the rest of their lives). Then, one starry night, it became time for – God's baby Son to be born. He would be God's perfect and holy Son on earth (because God was His Father), and He would be a man (because Mary was His mother).

You can read the amazing, true <u>Christ</u>mas story in the book of "Luke" in the Bible (the 2<sup>nd</sup> part of the Bible, called the New Testament). <u>Christ</u>mas is the holiday we celebrate to remember the birth of Jesus, also called the Christ. Did you know that? The baby's name would be Jesus, because the name Jesus means that He would save His people from their sins.

# 9

# Jesus Was Born

. . . . . and lived a life just like our life, with many happy events and with many sad events, <u>so He could know how it is down here for us and how hard it can be</u> when evil people hurt us and damage us. But He never let the evil people get Him down, because he always kept the "big picture" in front of Him. He wants us to do this too!

He was the only perfect man to walk this earth, because <u>He was God's ONLY perfect son, and because He was God He was able</u> to heal many people in pain and who had many diseases while He was here; He also healed some people who could not walk, talk, or see. He healed many people in their minds too. He even brought a really good friend of His, back to life again who had died several days before! He was kind, compassionate, and merciful — <u>people loved Him and were drawn to Him because He had such a great charisma</u>

<u>about Him.</u> He would be the man who arrived at the party, and every head would turn to notice Him – that kind of a man.

But the most important thing He did while He was here was to teach people about His Father, God, and <u>He was always focused on His job</u>. Teaching people about God is called "preaching" and he especially liked to preach – outside, go boating with his fishermen friends, and cook breakfast for his friends, on a campfire on the beach where they fished. He was definitely a man's man and an outdoorsman. So many people were always following Him just to be able to hear about God; so sometimes He would just stop when He saw a huge field before Him, and have the hundreds and sometimes thousands of people just all sit down in the field. Sometimes He even fed thousands of people who were following Him! On one such day, a little boy gave Jesus his small packed lunch with just some bread and fish in it. Jesus took the little boy's lunch, small as it was, and looked up to Heaven (just like you did at the beginning of the book), <u>and thanked His Father for it</u>. Then he had his friends begin passing out bread and fish to everyone seated in the field. Everyone was really hungry, because they had been walking a long time with Jesus, just so they could hear every word He had to tell them. (No McDonald's or fast food "drive-throughs" out there such a long time ago). BUT THE FOOD – NEVER RAN OUT. So his friends kept passing it out – to thousands - of people! Everyone had plenty to eat . . . still, the food never ran out! After everyone had eaten, his friends gathered up lots and lots of "left-overs"! Jesus told them to gather up all the left-overs, so that no food would be wasted! We shouldn't waste the food God gives us either, or anything else for that matter. Jesus doesn't want us to waste anything, especially our lives. This was just one of many, many miracles Jesus did while He was here on earth. He also went to a wedding reception party, and turned water into wine when all the wine ran out; He wanted to show the people that God had saved the best – for the last; not just the wine, but also Himself.

His closest friends who hung out with Him, and walked with Him from town to town while He preached – just knew that being with

Him – was way more important than working a job (to get more money). I think they knew they were not going to get to be with Him for very long, so they wanted to feel His love and compassion, and watch everything He did, and learn everything they could, that He had come to show and to tell them. They knew that this was the most important thing they could ever do – follow and "hang out" with Jesus. Besides, after He left to go back to Heaven, they could always get a job to get more money. Which was more important? Hanging out with Jesus or getting more money?

People were drawn to Him, and followed Him because they knew He was "different"; he was "different" because he was God here on earth. The evil people also recognized Him too . . . and because they were evil, they began to make plans . . . to kill Him . . . . . .

# 10

# But He Already Knew It

. . . . . because remember, that was the whole reason that God came down here. Came down here, to save us from our sins and to take our place when we die, so that we do not have to go to "the other place" called Hell. Hell was never made for people, only for the Devil, (also called Satan), and - his – angels (the evil angels). This is the place you DO NOT want to go, because this is where the Devil and his angels live along with all the people who choose him (and do evil), and not Jesus. These people are the Lord's enemies, and they also want to have YOUR heart; they try to get into your heart through bad music, drugs, alcohol, and bad sex. Even though the Lord never wanted anyone to have to go to Hell, they – will – go there by there own "free will", if they choose the Devil and not the Lord.

# 11

# And Die He Did

. . . . . a terrible death, when the evil people sent soldiers with spears to take Him to the place where they would kill Him. They spread out His arms and nailed His hands to a splintered rough wooden cross, then nailed His feet to the cross, and took most of His clothes off to shame Him. They spit on Him and humiliated Him . . . with many people watching their cruelty, who could do nothing to help Him against the soldiers. His good friend, Peter, tried to draw his sword to fight off the soldiers, but Jesus told him not to, because He HAD TO BE crucified because He loved us so much, and had to pay God's price for all our sins. His mother, Mary, was also there, while He was dying on the cross and I cannot even think about her pain and agony for her son. Jesus looked down on her and asked His close friend, John, to take care of His mother after He died, even though Mary had had other children after Jesus was born, with her husband, Joseph. He did not ask any of His relatives to take care of His mother – He asked the friend He loved so much, to take care of her, and John did.

The movie, "The Passion" (produced by Mel Gibson), shows what the crucifixion of the Lord Jesus Christ would have been like. You can see the movie to help you understand what Christ went through — for you, for me, and for all the rest of the world. When Christ died, He actually went down into Hell for us, so we would not have to go there when WE die. <u>HE WENT FOR US</u>. By doing all of this, <u>HE PAID THE PRICE for all the sins of the world, so that we could now be accepted by God</u>.

# 12

# But The Story Doesn't End Here

. . . . . because after 3 days, Jesus arose from the dead!!! to show us that HE HAD OVERCOME DEATH ITSELF — FOR US! After going to see His friends and showing them that He was truly alive again, He went back up – into the sky – home to the other side, and some of His closest friends got to see Him go up through the clouds! He told them before He went up into the sky, that He would come back to earth some day. I can't imagine why He would ever want to come back down here and re-live all the pain He went through; no one ever wants to go back to a place where they had to go through a lot of pain and suffering. . . . . . .

I feel sure they were all crying, because I am crying right now, just writing this all down for you, because I am absolutely overwhelmed by what Jesus did for me, and – for you.

He also told them something to comfort them, so that after He left them, they would not be so sad and cry, because they would miss Him so badly. He told them that when He arrived back home, His Father would send His very own heart (spirit) back down to us, <u>so that His spirit (in His heart) could come down here and live with us, and be inside our heart.</u>

<u>This way He could always be so very close to you and to me</u>

<u>by living INSIDE OUR HEARTS.</u>

# 13

# How?

If you pray this prayer, Jesus WILL come into your heart. Praying is just talking to Jesus, just like you would talk to a friend (because He IS the BEST friend you will ever have). Just talk quietly with these words from your mouth, and with these words in your heart. Just read this simple prayer quietly, but where you can actually hear yourself praying . . . . .

"Jesus Christ, I ask you to come into my heart. I ask you to forgive ALL my sins. Thank you with all my heart for dying – in my place, on the cross, and for going down into Hell IN MY PLACE for all my sins. I tell you now how very sorry I am for all of my sins. It should have been me on that cross, and not you.

Thank you that you rose from the dead and overcame death in my place. Thank you that now your Holy Spirit will live inside my heart and be always with me while I live – on this side – and when you call my name to end my days here on earth, You will carry my spirit up into Heaven to be with you forever. I will leave my old earthly body behind with all it's sadness and pain, and trade it in for a brand new one in Heaven when I come home. Thank you that you found me, and that I have found you. You are everything I have been looking for to fill my empty heart . . . . ."

# YOU ARE MY IT!

# 14

# Now

. . . . . that you have Jesus inside your heart, His spirit is called Holy (because it's perfect and without any sin) Spirit, or for short, HS. He is the most powerful spirit in all the world, and way more powerful than all the evil spirits put together, who belong to the devil. This is so important to know, so that you won't have to be so afraid anymore — <u>remember, this was the first wish at the beginning of the book</u>! He will ALWAYS be with you BECAUSE YOUR HEART GOES EVERYWHERE - YOU - GO. You can never leave your heart behind, can you? You will always have Him along. Never alone again at home, never alone at school or on the school bus, never alone at work (or with a "mean" supervisor if you have one), never alone at night. If you have a nightmare or bad dream, IF you say, "JESUS CHRIST" out loud, the evil spirits giving you the bad dream will run away, BECAUSE THEY KNOW HS is the most powerful spirit and they are afraid of Him! He will protect you from danger and if something really bad happens to you, and you should die, HE WILL carry you straight up to Heaven.

He will help you get through all the hard stuff down here and help you know what to do – if you pray – and ask Him. LISTEN to Him in your heart. It's the knowing what to do in your heart and mind, but the knowing got there through a different circuit. You will not hear your answers through your ear, like someone talking to you whose human voice you can hear. HS, remember is a spirit (not a man) who talks to us in "a still small voice" (inside our spirit, inside our heart). You will hear your answers in this way - through the HS circuit.

Read The Holy Bible a lot too, because it is "God's Instruction Manual". It tells you what to do in order for God's product to work best, and also tells you how to do the "maintenance" part so that His product will last longer. It will also tell you what to do in confusing situations and tell you amazing stories about other people who lived before you - and all the amazing things

God did for them. What he did for them, HE WILL DO FOR YOU. You will want to read these books ahead, so that you will know ahead of time, what to do in your own life. THE BIBLE - IS GOD'S AND JESUS' WORDS BACK TO YOU! You can read the paper copy of the manual, or like they tell you (when you buy a new electronic product now) - you have to read it "on-line" and print a copy off - if you want one. If you don't have a book copy of The Bible, you can read it on-line! and you don't even have to have a special "app".

Even though we cannot understand everything in the Bible, we CAN UNDERSTAND the parts we need to know about. If we could understand all of it, we would be as smart as God, and we all know that that would be absolutely impossible!

You can begin reading the books of "Matthew", "Mark," "Luke", and "John" in the 2nd part of the Bible (the 1st part is the Old Testament and the 2nd part is the New Testament). Matthew is the first book of the New Testament and begins like www.ancestry.com – to prove that Jesus was really here on earth as a man, with ancestry that can be traced. Of course, there is no www.ancestry.com for God because He has always been God, and way before he ever made anything or anyone down here!

# 15

# We Aren't Here
# For Very Long

. . . . . and I hate to tell you this, BUT THE CLOCK IS TICKING AWAY!!! "Your clock", that is! Because the number of days you get to be down here – has already been determined. The One who made us and put us here is the ONLY ONE who knows how many days we get to be here. AND He has already factored in the choices we will make before we die – how many surgeries we will choose to have, whether or not we take chemo, wars we are called upon to fight in (and perhaps die in), and any other "heroic medical measures" we (or our caregiver) decide upon. Some people do not want "heroic measures" or to be resuscitated and are ready to go home and be with Christ. Other people want to stay down here for as long as they possibly can, and because The Lord has given us "free will" to choose, all of our choices are factored in - ahead of time.

Our choices always affect many people. If our choices are not good, the outcomes will also not be good, and the bad outcomes could have been avoided altogether IF our prayers had been, "thy will be done on earth, as it is in Heaven".

Sometimes a person dies quickly, without their getting to make any choices at all about when they die, like a heart attack or a car accident, or if they are shot to death. But this way they do not have to suffer and be in a lot of pain that their choices might have given them – later on – if they die quickly.

So, there are many reasons why people die, at different times, and why some are young and some are old. People often say they do not understand "why" a person they love is "taken away from them" – sooner than they wanted. And yet sometimes, God saves people a lot of pain and suffering when He takes them to Heaven at a younger age, because ONLY HE knows their futures and what their lives would have been like if they lived to be old. One thing to be sure of though, is that God knows ALL of these things — ahead of time. AND - HE - DECIDES THE FINAL DAY.

In Heaven, there will not be "free will" because ONLY the Lord's will - is done in Heaven. This is why the words in the "Lord's Prayer" (the Lord taught us to pray) say, "thy will be done ON EARTH AS IT IS IN HEAVEN", because God's will is too often NOT DONE HERE ON EARTH. We are told to pray this way, clearly, BECAUSE His will is most often – not done here on earth.

Soooooo . . . . . DO YOU REALLY THINK IT IS GOD'S WILL ON EARTH - FOR YOU - to spend MOST of your time down here — on your phone and I-Pad, just playing games that are all

PRETEND ? ? ?

## How much time do you think you have already lost?

Be sure – YOU CAN NEVER GET BACK – THE TIME YOU HAVE ALREADY LOST. TIME IS NOT FOR SALE, NOT EVEN ON AMAZON, WHO SELLS THINGS THAT YOU CANNOT BUY ANYWHERE ELSE. YOUR PARENTS CANNOT USE THEIR CREDIT CARDS TO BUY SOMETHING SO IMPORTANT FOR YOU, even though they can buy you all kinds of other stuff . . . . .

Just maybe, it would be a good idea to pray and read the Bible and ask Jesus what he and His Dad's plan for your life was, when they made you in the beginning. DO YOU THINK???

Wouldn't it just be sooooo sad IF YOU got to the end of your life and you had never become and had never done what you had been divinely designed to do? And all because you didn't take the time to find out. You didn't find out BECAUSE you used up all that precious time (you needed to find out) to play those stupid games. Time you can never get back.

No matter the price in dollars you or your
parents might be willing to pay. . . . .

## TIME IS NOT FOR SALE!

. . . . . . . . So always be
remembering . . . . . . . .

"We aren't here for very long."

# 16

# Problems

. . . . . are everywhere down here, and there are lots of them; no, not lots of them, way more than lots of them. When you are younger, you think that you are the ONLY one to have them. WRONG! Everyone, yes, everyone has way more than lots of problems — rich people, poor people, handsome and beautiful people, plain looking people, old people, young people, hard working people, "people who don't have to work" people, and all the other people you would never imagine would have any problems at all.

What to do with a problem? First of all, it's a good idea to pray and ask the Lord to help you get your problem fixed. It's really important to know that you can't fix all of your problems all by yourself, depending on what kind of problem it is. But, if you can fix it, you need to try and fix it right away, and as soon as you can, BECAUSE IT IS NOT GOING AWAY!

"Homework" would be a good example. Some people think that if they ignore the problem, it will just go away. WRONG AGAIN! So, trust me, the sooner you can fix your problem, the sooner it will go away. Now here is the hard part – if you can't fix it all by yourself (like your car), then you must take it to an auto mechanic repair place AND PAY YOUR HARD EARNED MONEY TO SOMEONE ELSE that you really do not want to give it to! But then again, if you have gotten a job because you need money, you can't get - to your job – without a car. Don't think for one minute that your friends will be more than happy to take you to work and pick you up every day; that would last for maybe up to 2 days max. So, you decide you HAVE TO pay the money to get your car fixed, and you get it fixed. But getting your car fixed creates another problem – now you can't quit your job you wanted to quit! because it took most of your money you'd earned and saved up, to pay for the car repairs! You were so hoping you could find a better job, one that would pay more money and with a nicer supervisor! The new problem is that you have to keep working at your old job with less money and with your mean supervisor, the one who watches you closely, hoping that you will make a mistake, so he or she can fire you! This is now an even worse problem to have, feeling that you can never escape! However, you decide to just stay put at your old job, until you can take PTO (earned vacation time off) to look for a better job. This, at least gives you some hope that you can escape, eventually. Besides, less money is better than no money at all, if you quit!

Also, it's a good idea not to "call in" and say that you are "sick", while you go and look for another job, because chances are that you will "run into" someone you work with, who IS "off" on their PTO, and you can be sure they – will tell – your supervisor that you lied, when you called in to work "sick" to get the time off! Now you have another problem, because you were planning on taking a nice vacation with your PTO, but now you have to use most of it up - to look for another job! This has also created another big problem – trying to get your money back on your vacation plane ticket! "Rots of ruck" (lots of luck) on that, because your plane ticket you bought "on-line" is NON-REFUNDABLE!

But here's the good news; you now have your car up and running so you can go and look for a better job when you can get enough PTO! Now is a good time – to laugh! because laughing helps a lot in this life! The Bible says that a merry heart does good, just like medicine.

There are tons of answers in the Bible to help us solve our problems, trust me, you will be amazed ! at all the answers to be found there. Praying is powerful and always helps a lot too, AND paying close attention to what you know HS is telling you to do. HS will also have other people tell you things you need to know, and they will not even know that what they are telling you is information that- the Lord- is giving you. A person, trying to hurt you, thinks they have hidden their plan well, but HS will reveal to you things that are being done against you, "secret things" that other people are doing to you that you would have never known about. Because Hs is taking care of you, you will find out these things in unusual ways, that you would not have known at all. So pay careful attention to what HS is telling you. He is always watching your back and protecting you.

It is also really important to know that you can learn SO MUCH from "older people", who have lived through a ton of life more than you have. They have learned how to fix soooo many problems. But they are NOT willing to share how to fix YOUR problems, IF you act all arrogant and "look down" on them like they are just old and stupid, just because you may know more about electronic devices than they do. Keep in mind this is probably the ONLY area that you may know more about. BUT IF you are humble, and ask them for their advice, almost always they will be willing to help you. The one thing that you should never do with other people, including people with disabilities, is act like you are sooo much smarter than they are, especially if you are only really smart in the one area of electronic devices. You can be proud and arrogant and "talk down" to other people, but be prepared to spend all your hard earned money – paying other people to fix all your problems – all the other ones you know nothing about. This means both at home and school, and, at work. It's always a good idea to just stay "humble" all the time and with everyone, BECAUSE YOU NEVER KNOW when you might need THEIR help.

So, now you know the best things to do to fix your problems: Pray, listen to HS, read the "Instruction Manual" (Bible), pay attention and listen to how the Lord is showing you things in most unusual ways, and go to people you can trust to help you figure out how to best solve your problems, if you cannot figure them out by yourself. IT'S ALWAYS BEST NOT TO TALK ABOUT YOUR PROBLEMS TO OTHER PEOPLE, ESPECIALLY AT WORK! THEY DON'T CARE AND ARE MORE CONCERNED WITH THEIR OWN PROBLEMS. IT ALSO MAKES YOU LOOK WEAK AND "WHINY". Even if they are "nosey", and act like they are really concerned about you, DO NOT share your problems with them. Chances are they would tell a lot of other people too. You should only talk to people you trust and can actually help you with your problem. And rarely, you will find one or two people you work with, who can help you figure out work problems, and maybe even personal problems; but be really careful what you tell other people. What you tell other people can really come back and "bite you".

ALWAYS REMEMBER to be respectful and NEVER, NEVER "look down" on other people, even if they are different than you, and not dressed as nice as you.

We need to always REMEMBER to say "thank you" to the Lord for all His help with our many problems; we SHOULD THANK HIM every time He helps us – this would mean that we are – always – thanking Him. Just a whispered "thank you" will make the Lord happy. One of HS' names is "the Helper" and you can certainly see why!

And — we always need to REMEMBER to tell the Lord Jesus how sorry we are when we screw up and do bad things (our sins), which we will do too many times. But when we remember all Jesus went through for us, we will remember how terrible our sins are to Him, and remembering this will help us NOT WANT TO SIN, which will save us a lot of grief in our futures.

These are all important things
to know and remember.

# 17

# Never Never Never
# Let Other People

. . . . . pressure you into doing what HS is warning you — NOT TO DO! This can be a mean supervisor, a relative, someone you work with, a teacher, a pastor or priest, someone you thought was your friend, a girl friend, a boy friend, or anyone pressuring you to do what you know is wrong. HS always "has your back" and He is always on your side. The worst mistakes I have made in my life – have been because – I listened to other people, and gave in to the pressure they put on me, to do things that HS was warning me NOT TO DO. When we disobey HS, who is always wanting to protect us, we must carry our bad choices, sometimes for the rest of our lives down here on earth. For myself, there is never a day in my life that I do not have physical pain in my body – for not listening to HS, and I imagine that I will always have this problem. This pain can be in your body, as in my case, or in your heart, or in both. Giving in to other people who want to control us, when we know better because of HS, always has a bad outcome for us. Sometimes other people can pressure us to do what - they - think is our duty or responsibility. If we listen to other people, and not to HS, we - will - suffer the consequences.

We "give in" because we are "people pleasers" and we hope that IF we do what they tell us to, then they will like us and accept us. Their pressure on us might also be to do drugs, alcohol, sex if you aren't married, which could result in your getting pregnant (or getting someone else pregnant), have an abortion (even though you could save your baby's life by carrying it, and giving it to someone else who could "adopt" it and love it). Other pressures could be for you to join a gang, steal money, lie, even kill other people, or any number of other things people pressure us into. IS THEIR APPROVAL REALLY WORTH IT???

I THINK NOT!!!

Remember, the 2nd wish at the beginning of your book, is to wish that you would not be so worried about what other people think about you. NOW you know that it's NOT worth the price you must pay.

AND NOW YOU KNOW about Holy Spirit, Jesus, and our Father who is in Heaven, so you no longer have to be so afraid (the 1st wish), or worry so much about dying (the 3rd wish). I also believe that our pets we love so much, will also be up in Heaven, because the Bible says that in Heaven, the lion will lay down with the lamb. Lions and lambs are animals :).

# 18

# When You Are So Sad

. . . . . the only place to go is to the Lord through His HS. He will comfort you and tell you deep down in your heart — what to do, so you won't have to feel so sad. Just talking to Him makes you feel better, and it's OK to cry when you are talking to Him. It's always a good idea to have some Kleenex or a paper towel handy when you are sad and talking to Him. If you're not even sure why you feel so sad, HS will even pray for you, when you really don't know how to pray or what to say - for yourself (or someone else you are trying to pray for). He will take over and pray for you. <u>No phone, I-Pad, or any other latest electrical gadget – or other person – can do this for you.</u>

<u>It's really important to know where to go, when you need help!</u>

Asking is praying, and receiving (answers) is from reading the Bible and listening to HS deep down in your heart.

Don't ever forget — where to go — to find your way when you are confused, when you are sad, when you are in danger, when you need answers.

It's really important to know where to go.

# 19

# And Now You Know

. . . . . that your phone, your I-Pad, and the "pretend games" you play on them . . . . .

can NEVER be. . . . .

# YOUR "IT"

# 20

# Jesus Did Everything

. . . . . His Father wanted Him to do with His life while He was down here, and He did it all in just 33 years. God is our Heavenly Father too, because He made us too.

Will I get everything done in my life time that God put me down here to do?

# Will you?

To Contact The Author,

Please write:

**sushan_davis@yahoo.com**